Impressum
Verlag: BABADADA GmbH, Nedderfeld 112 , 22529 Hamburg
Geschäftsführer / Verlagsleitung: Harald Hof
Druck: Books on Demand GmbH, In de Tarpen 42, 22848 Norderstedt

Imprint
Publisher: BABADADA GmbH, Nedderfeld 112 , 22529 Hamburg, Germany
Managing Director / Publishing direction: Harald Hof
Print: Books on Demand GmbH, In de Tarpen 42, 22848 Norderstedt

المدرسة

school

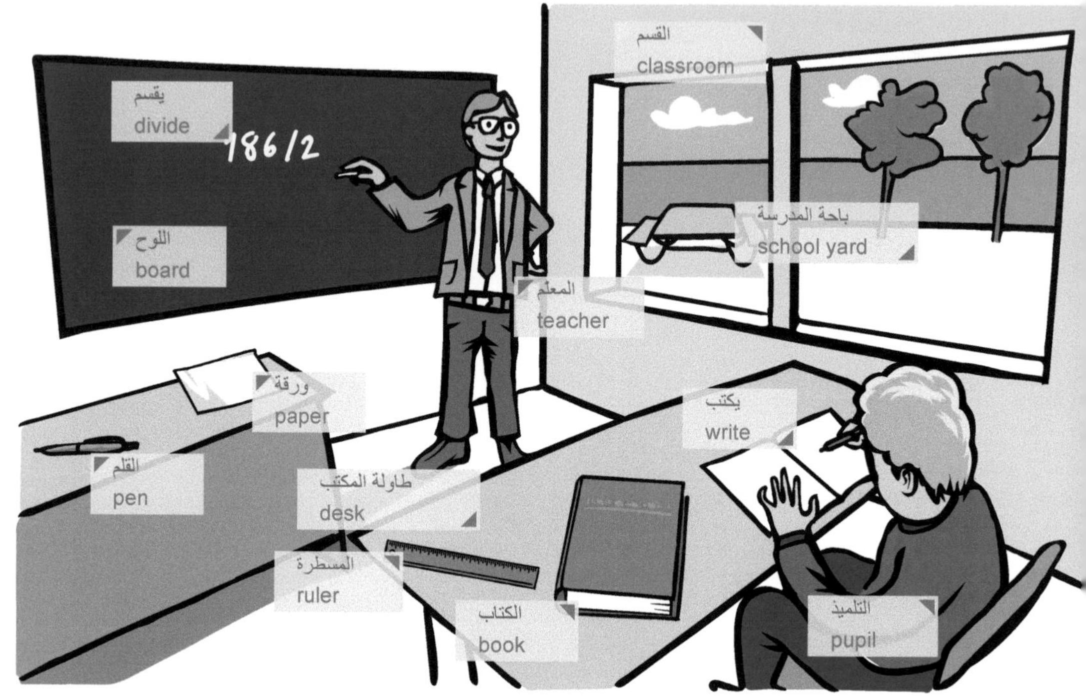

القسم
classroom
يقسم
divide
186/2
اللوح
board
باحة المدرسة
school yard
المعلم
teacher
ورقة
paper
يكتب
write
القلم
pen
طاولة المكتب
desk
المسطرة
ruler
الكتاب
book
التلميذ
pupil

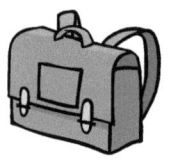

الحقيبة المدرسية

satchel

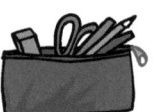

المقلمة

pencil case

قلم الرصاص

pencil

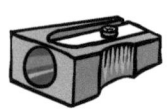

البرّاية

pencil sharpener

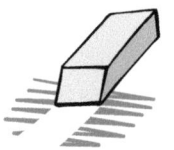

المِمحاة

rubber

دفتر الرسم

drawing pad

الرسمة

drawing

الفرشاة

paintbrush

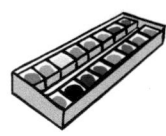

علبة التلوين

paint box

المقص

scissors

المادة اللاصقة

glue

دفتر التمارين

exercise book

الواجب المدرسي

homework

الرقم

number

يجمع

add

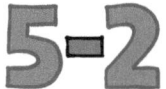

يطرح

subtract

يضرب

multiply

يحسب

calculate

الحرف

letter

الأبجدية

alphabet

كلمة

word

النص

text

يقرأ

read

الطبشور

chalk

الحصة

lesson

دفتر الدوام المدرسي

register

الامتحان

exam

شهادة

certificate

اللباس المدرسي

school uniform

التعليم

education

الموسوعة

encyclopedia

الجامعة

university

المجهر

microscope

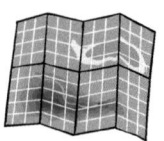

الخريطة

map

قماما

waste-paper basket

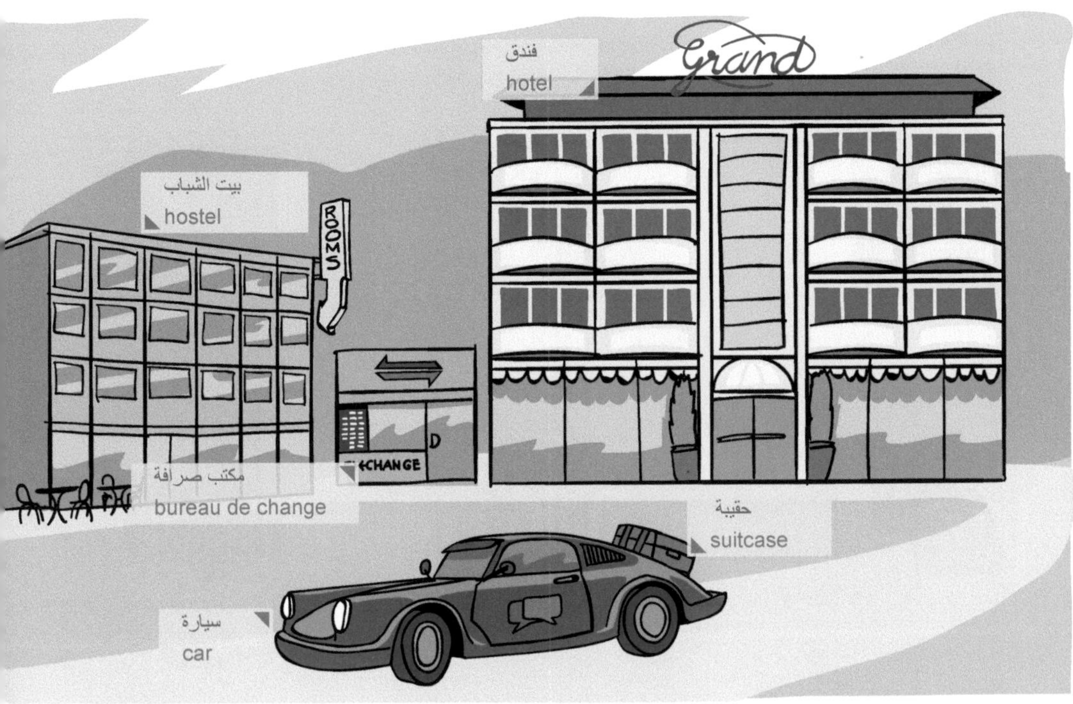
فندق
hotel
Grand
بيت الشباب
hostel
ROOMS
CHANGE
مكتب صرافة
bureau de change
حقيبة
suitcase
سيارة
car

اللغة

language

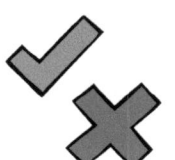

نعم / لا

yes / no

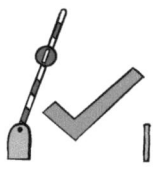

حسناً

Okay

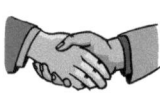

مرحباً

hello

مترجم

translator

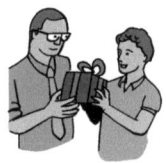

شكراً

Thank you

كم ثمن ... ؟

how much is…?

لا أفهم

I do not understand

مشكلة

problem

مساء الخير

Good evening!

صباح الخير!

Good morning!

ليلة سعيدة

Good night!

إلى اللقاء

bye bye

اتجاه

direction

أمتعة السفر

luggage

حقيبة

bag

حقيبة ظهر

backpack

ضيف

guest

غرفة

room

كيس للنوم

sleeping bag

خيمة

tent

استعلامات سياحية

tourist information

شاطئ

beach

بطاقة ائتمان

credit card

إفطار

breakfast

طعام الغداء

lunch

العشاء

dinner

بطاقة سفر

ticket

مصعد

lift

طابع بريدي

stamp

حدود

border

الجمارك

customs

سفارة

embassy

تأشيرة

visa

جواز سفر

passport

نقل

transport

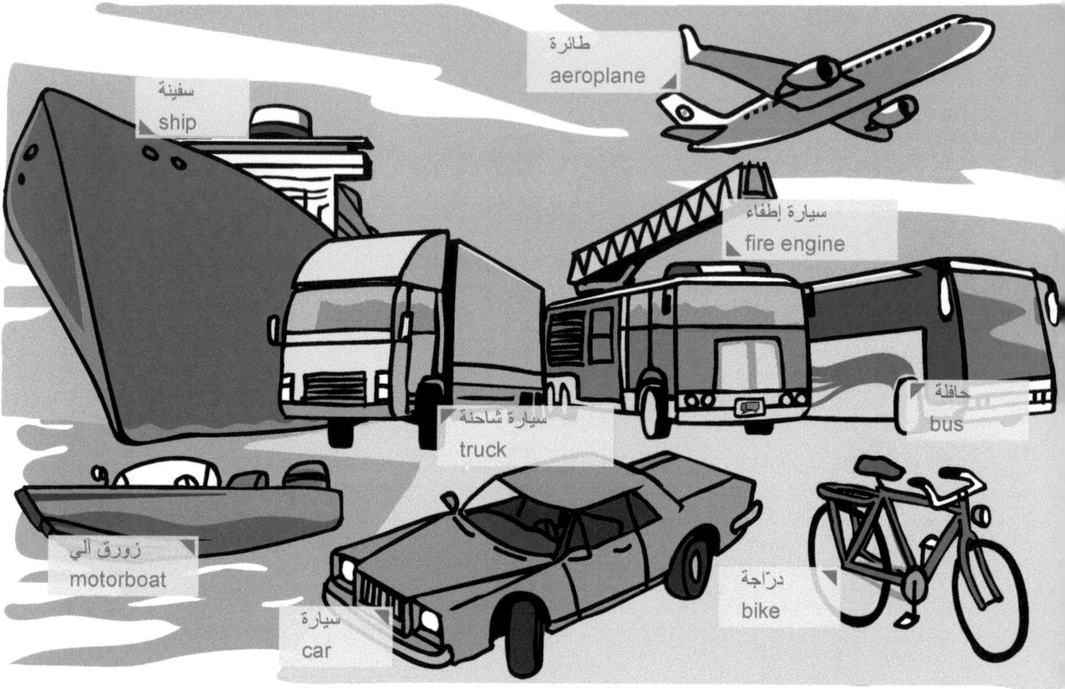

طائرة
aeroplane
سفينة
ship
سيارة إطفاء
fire engine
حافلة
bus
سيارة شاحنة
truck
زورق آلي
motorboat
درّاجة
bike
سيارة
car

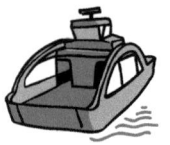

عبارة

ferry

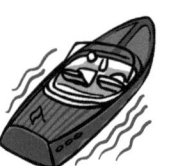

قارب

boat

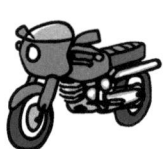

دراجة نارية

motorbike

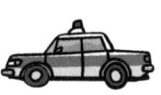

سيارة شرطة

police car

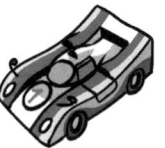

سيارة سباق

racing car

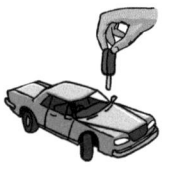

سيارة مستأجرة

rental car

أسلوب تشاركي في استئجار السيارات

car sharing

سيارة للجر

breakdown truck

سيارة نقل القمامة

refuse truck

محرك

motor

وقود

fuel

محطة وقود

petrol station

إشارة مرور

traffic sign

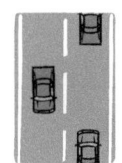

حركة السير

traffic

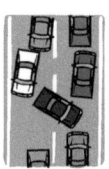

ازدحام سير

traffic jam

موقف سيارات

car park

محطة قطار

train station

سكك حديدية

tracks

قطار

train

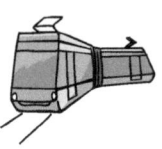

ترام

tram

عربة قطار

carriage

طائرة مروحية

helicopter

مطار

airport

برج

tower

مسافر

passenger

حاوية

container

علبة كرتون

carton

عربة يد

cart

سلة

basket

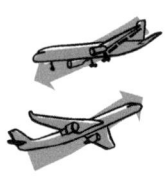

يقلع / يهبط

take off / land

مدينة

city

قرية

village

مركز المدينة

city centre

بيت

house

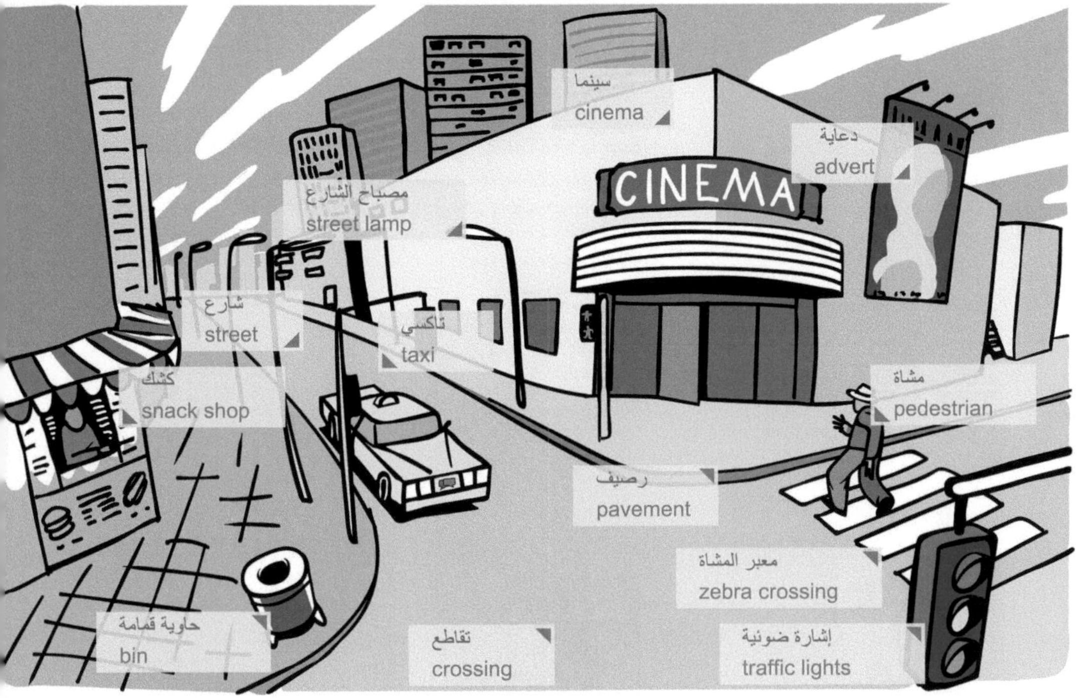
سينما
cinema
دعاية
advert
CINEMA
مصباح الشارع
street lamp
شارع
street
تاكسي
taxi
كشك
snack shop
مشاة
pedestrian
رصيف
pavement
معبر المشاة
zebra crossing
حاوية قمامة
bin
تقاطع
crossing
إشارة ضوئية
traffic lights

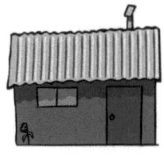

كوخ

hut

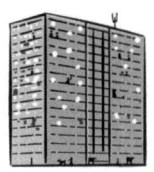

شقة

flat

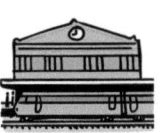

محطة قطار

train station

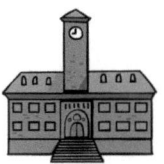

دار البلدية

town hall

MUSEUM

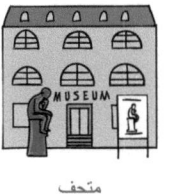

متحف

museum

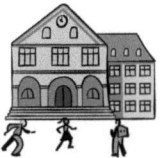

المدرسة

school

الجامعة

university

مصرف

bank

المستشفى

hospital

فندق

hotel

صيدلية

pharmacy

مكتب

office

مكتبة

book shop

متجر

shop

محل لبيع الزهور

florist's

سوبرماركت

supermarket

سوق

market

متجر كبير

department store

تاجر السمك

fishmonger's

مركز تسوّق

shopping centre

ميناء

harbour

حديقة عامة

park

مقعد

bench

جسر

bridge

درج، سلم

stairs

مترو

underground

نفق

tunnel

موقف حافلات

bus stop

بار

bar

مطعم

restaurant

صندوق البريد

postbox

لافتة باسم الشارع

street sign

مقياس زمن الوقوف

parking meter

حديقة حيوانات

zoo

مسبح

swimming pool

مسجد

mosque

مزرعة
farm

تلوث البيئة
pollution

مقبرة
graveyard

كنيسة
church

ملعب الأطفال
playground

معبد
temple

طبيعة ريفية

landscape

ورقة
leaf

علامة إرشاد
signpost

طريق
way

مرج
meadow

حجر
stone

شجرة
tree

رحالة
hiker

نهر
river

عشب
grass

زهرة
flower

وادٍ

valley

جبل

hill

بحيرة

lake

غابة

forest

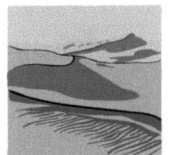

صحراء

desert

بركان

volcano

قلعة

castle

قوس قزح

rainbow

فطر

mushroom

نخلة

palm tree

بعوض

mosquito

ذبابة

fly

نملة

ant

نحلة

bee

عنكبوت

spider

خنفساء

beetle

ضفدعة

frog

سنجاب

squirrel

قنفذ

hedgehog

أرنب

hare

بومة

owl

عصفور

bird

بجعة

swan

خنزير برّي

boar

غزال

deer

إلكة

moose

سد

dam

دولاب الطاحونة الهوائية

wind turbine

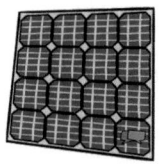

خلية شمسية

solar panel

مناخ

climate

مطعم

restaurant

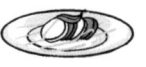

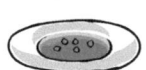

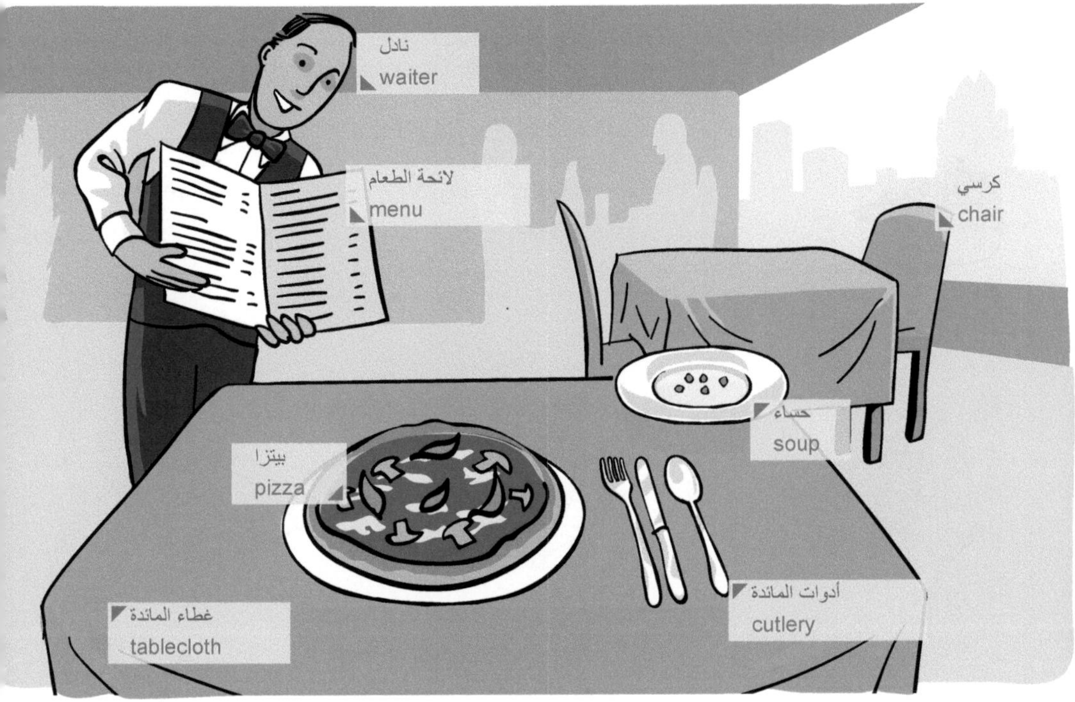

نادل
waiter
لائحة الطعام
menu
كرسي
chair
حساء
soup
بيتزا
pizza
أدوات المائدة
cutlery
غطاء المائدة
tablecloth

مقبلات

starter

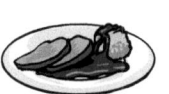

الصحن الرئيسي

main course

حلوى أو فاكهة بعد الطعام

dessert

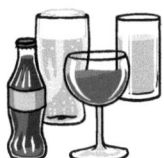

مشروبات

drinks

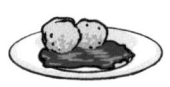

طعام

food

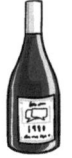

زجاجة

bottle

وجبات سريعة

fast food

طعام الشارع

street food

إبريق الشاي

teapot

علبة السكر

sugar bowl

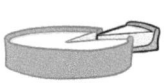

حصّة

portion

آلة الإسبريسو

espresso machine

كرسي عالٍ

high chair

فاتورة

bill

صينية

tray

سكين

knife

شوكة

fork

ملعقة

spoon

ملعقة الشاي

teaspoon

منديل المائدة

serviette

كأس

glass

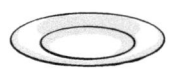

صحن
....
plate

صحن الحساء
....
soup plate

صحن الفنجان
....
saucer

صلصة
....
sauce

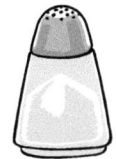

مملحة
....
salt pot

مطحنة الفلفل
....
pepper mill

خلّ
....
vinegar

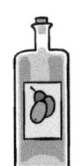

زيت الطعام
....
oil

توابل
....
spices

كتشاب
....
ketchup

خردل
....
mustard

مايونيز
....
mayonnaise

سوبرماركت

supermarket

عرض خاص
special offer
FOR
زبون
customer
مشتقات الحليب
dairy
فواكه
fruit
عربة تسوّق
trolley

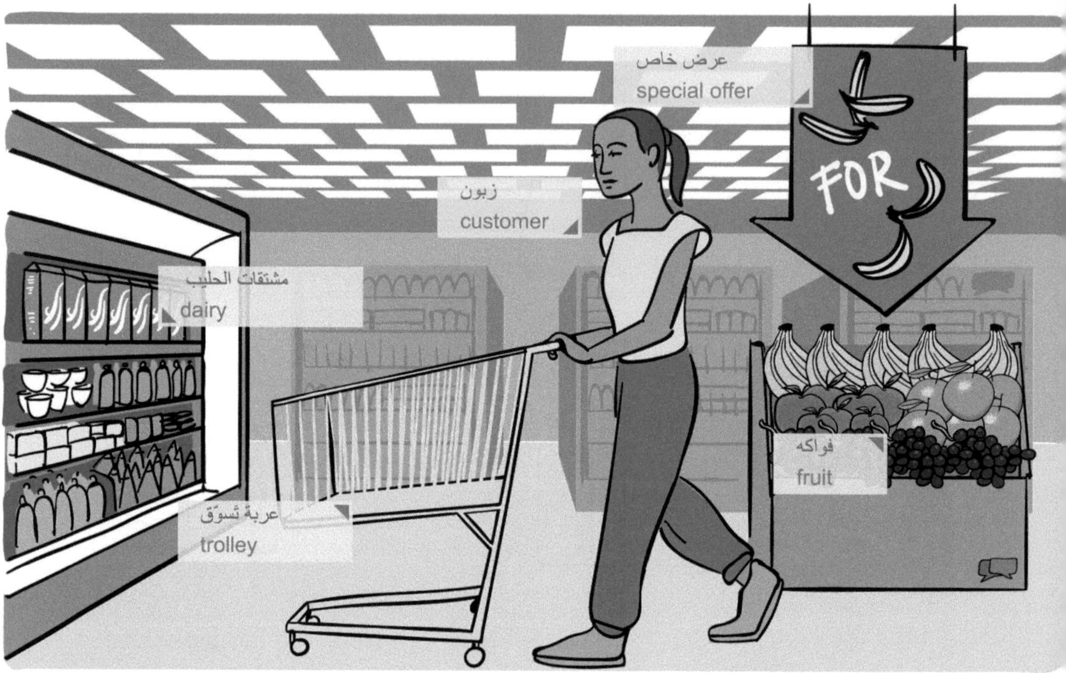

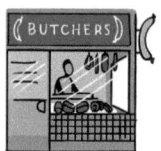

BUTCHERS

جزّار

butcher´s

BAKERY

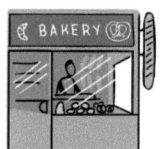

مخبز

baker´s

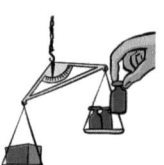

يزن

weigh

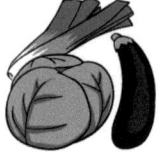

خضار

vegetables

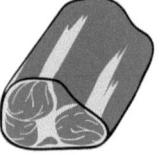

لحم

meat

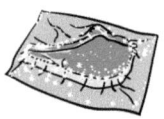

المأكولات المجمّدة

frozen food

مرتدلا أو جبن

cold meat

معلّبات

tinned food

مسحوق الغسيل

washing powder

حلويات

sweets

المواد المنزلية

household products

منظّفات

cleaning products

بائعة

salesperson

صندوق الحساب

till

أمين صندوق

cashier

قائمة المشتريات

shopping list

أوقات العمل

opening hours

محفظة النقود

wallet

بطاقة ائتمان

credit card

حقيبة

bag

كيس بلاستيكي

plastic bag

ماء

water

عصير

juice

حليب

milk

كولا

coke

نبيذ

wine

بيرة

beer

كحول

alcohol

كاكاو

cocoa

شاي

tea

قهوة

coffee

قهوة إسبريسو

espresso

كابوتشينو

cappuccino

موزة

banana

تفاح

apple

برتقال

orange

بطيخ

melon

ليمون

lemon

جزرة

carrot

ثوم

garlic

خيزران

bamboo

بصل

onion

فطر

mushroom

لوزيات

nuts

شعيرية

noodles

سباغيتي

spaghetti

أرزّ

rice

سلطة

salad

بطاطا مقلية

chips

بطاطا مقلية

fried potatoes

بيتزا

pizza

هامبورغر

hamburger

ساندويش

sandwich

شريحة لحم مقلية

cutlet

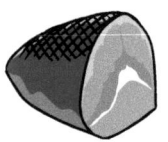

لحم خنزير

ham

سلامي

salami

سجق

sausage

دجاج

chicken

لحم محمر

roast

سمك

fish

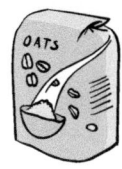

دقيق الشوفان

porridge oats

موسلي

muesli

كورن فلكس

cornflakes

طحين

flour

كرواسان

croissant

خبز صغير

bread roll

خبز

bread

خبز محمص

toast

بسكويت

biscuits

زبدة

butter

لبن زبادي

curd

كعكة

cake

بيضة

egg

بيض مقلي

fried egg

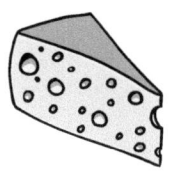

جبنة

cheese

مثلجات

ice cream

سكر

sugar

عسل

honey

مربّى الفاكهة

jam

كريم النوغا

chocolate spread

الكاري

curry

مزرعة

farm

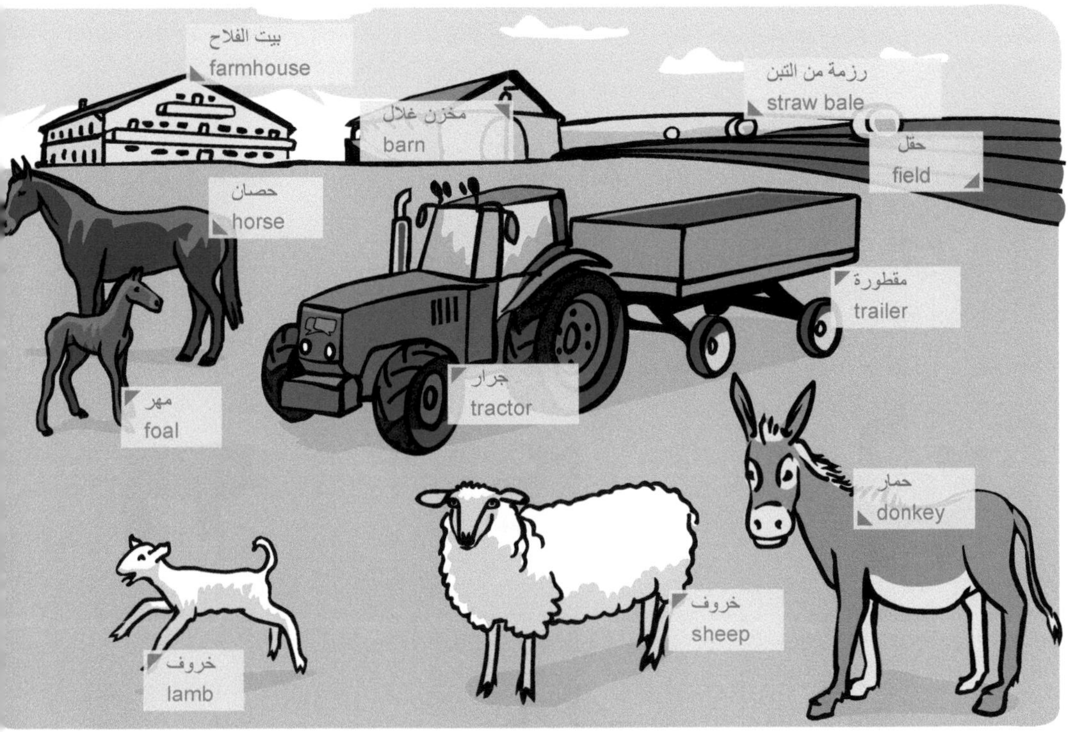

بيت الفلاح
farmhouse
مخزن غلال
barn
رزمة من التبن
straw bale
حقل
field
حصان
horse
مقطورة
trailer
جرار
tractor
مهر
foal
حمار
donkey
خروف
sheep
خروف
lamb

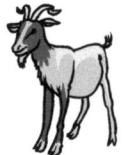

ماعز
....
goat

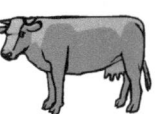

بقرة
....
cow

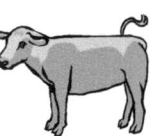

عجل
....
calf

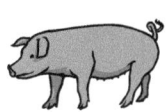

خنزير
....
pig

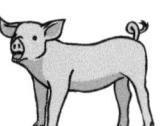

خنزير صغير
....
piglet

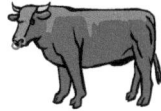

ثور
....
bull

إوزّة

goose

بطة

duck

صوص

chick

دجاجة

hen

ديك

cock

جرذ

rat

قطة

cat

فأر

mouse

ثور

ox

كلب

dog

كوخ الكلب

doghouse

خرطوم الحديقة

garden hose

إبريق

watering can

منجل

scythe

المحراث

plough

منجل

sickle

معزقة

hoe

مذراة الزبل

pitchfork

بلطة

axe

عربة يد

wheelbarrow

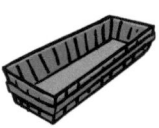

معلف

trough

صفيحة الحليب

milk can

كيس

sack

سياج

fence

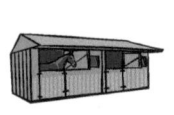

اصطبل

stable

دفيئة

greenhouse

تربة

soil

بذور

seed

سماد

fertilizer

حصّادة درّاسة

combine harvester

يحصد

harvest

محصول

harvest

بطاطا يامس

yams

قمح

wheat

صويا

soy

بطاطا

potato

ذرة

corn

سلجم

rapeseed

شجرة فاكهة

fruit tree

نبات منيهوت

cassava

الحبوب

cereals

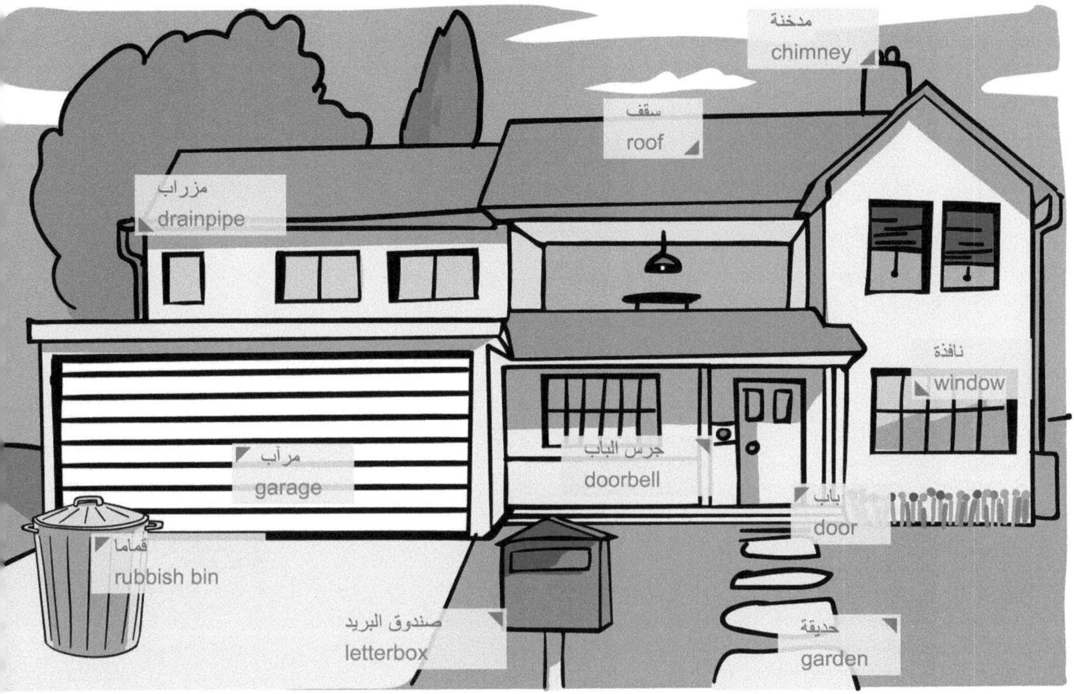

house

مدخنة
chimney

سقف
roof

مزراب
drainpipe

نافذة
window

مرآب
garage

جرس الباب
doorbell

باب
door

قماما
rubbish bin

صندوق البريد
letterbox

حديقة
garden

غرفة جلوس
living room

الحمّام
bathroom

مطبخ
kitchen

غرفة النوم
bedroom

غرفة الأطفال
child's room

غرفة الطعام
dining room

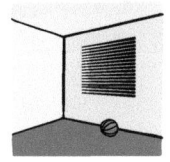

أرضية

floor

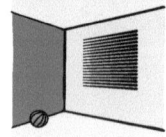

حائط

wall

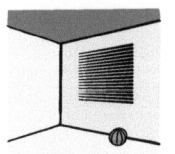

سقف

ceiling

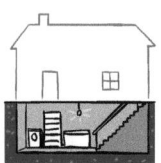

قبو

cellar

ساونا

sauna

بلكون

balcony

شرفة

terrace

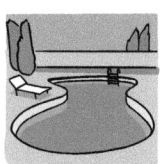

مسبح

pool

جزّازة العشب

lawn mower

بياضات السرير

sheet

بطانية

bedspread

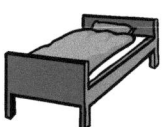

سرير

bed

مكنسة

broom

سطل

bucket

مفتاح كهربائي

switch

غرفة جلوس
living room

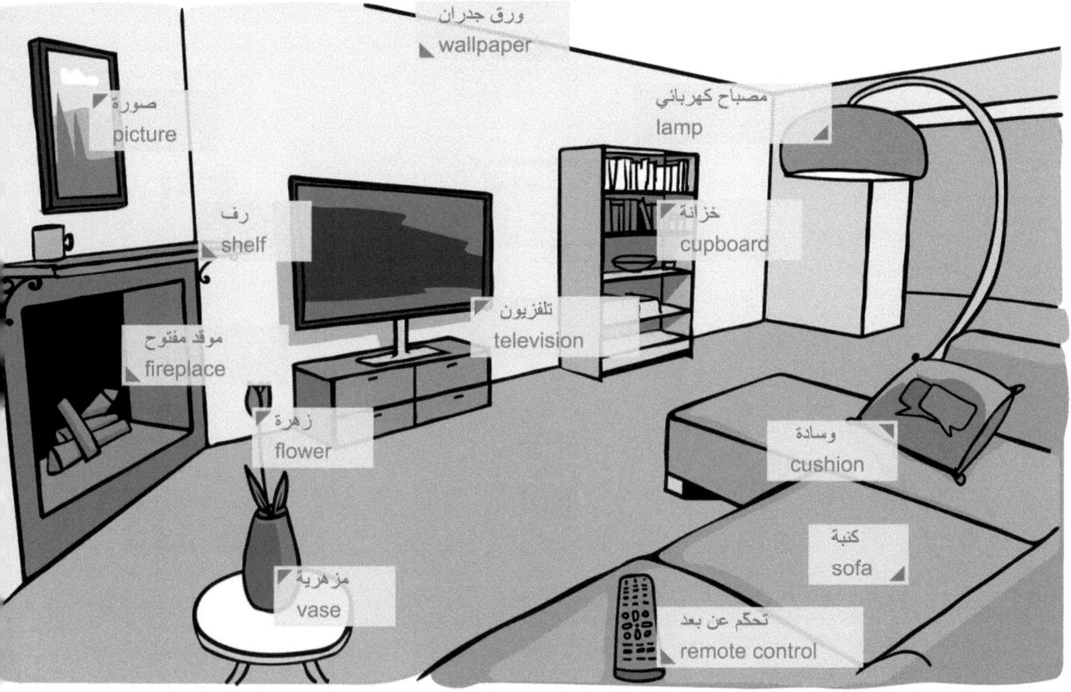

ورق جدران
wallpaper
صورة
picture
مصباح كهربائي
lamp
رف
shelf
خزانة
cupboard
تلفزيون
television
موقد مفتوح
fireplace
زهرة
flower
وسادة
cushion
كنبة
sofa
مزهرية
vase
تحكم عن بعد
remote control

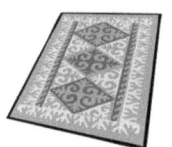

بصاط

carpet

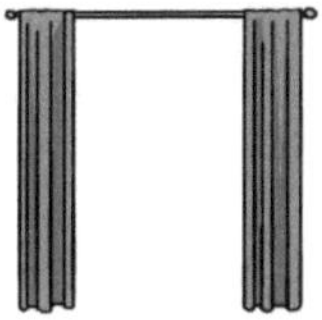

ستارة

curtain

طاولة

table

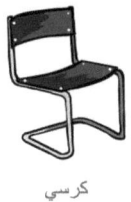

كرسي

chair

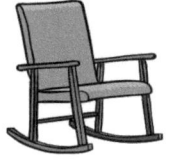

كرسي هزّاز

rocking chair

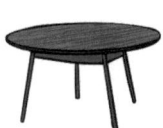

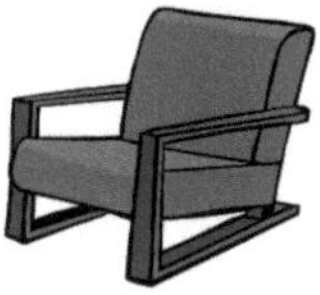

كرسي ذو ذراعين

armchair

الكتاب

book

بطّانية

blanket

زخرفة

decoration

الحطب

firewood

فيلم

film

تجهيزات ستيريو

hi-fi equipment

مفتاح

key

جريدة

newspaper

لوحة مرسومة

painting

مُلصق

poster

راديو

radio

دفتر ملاحظات

notepad

المكنسة الكهربائية

hoover

صبّار

cactus

شمعة

candle

مطبخ

kitchen

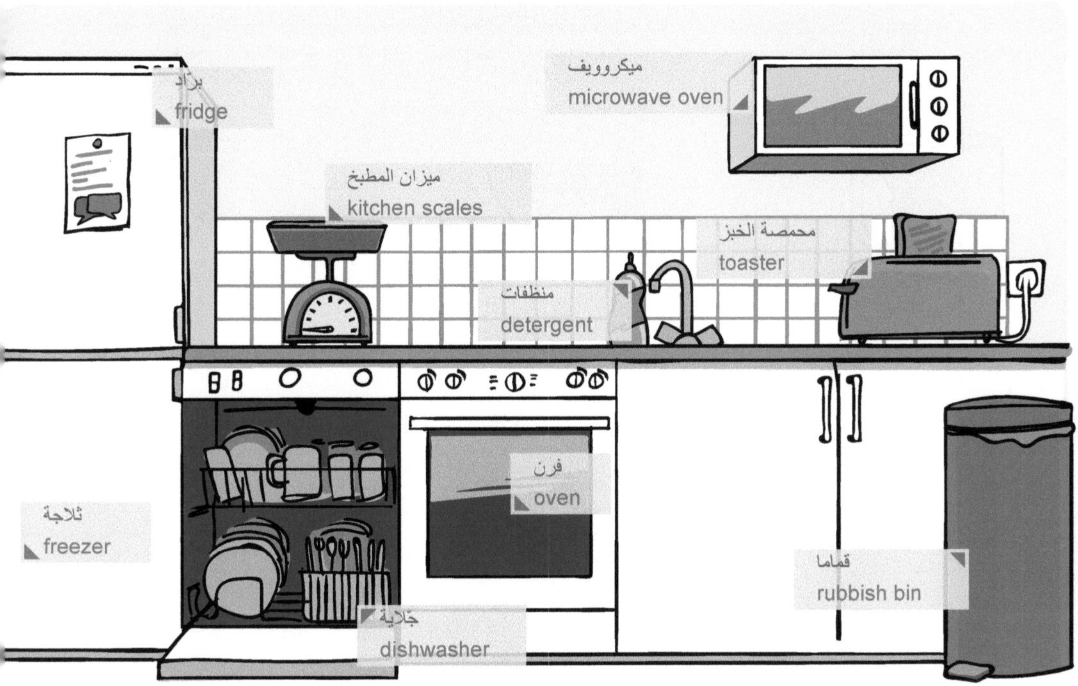

براد
fridge
ميكروويف
microwave oven
ميزان المطبخ
kitchen scales
محمصة الخبز
toaster
منظفات
detergent
فرن
oven
ثلاجة
freezer
قماما
rubbish bin
جَلاية
dishwasher

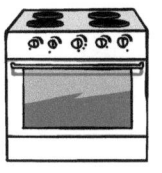

موقد

cooker

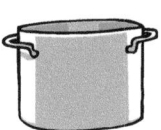

قِدر

pot

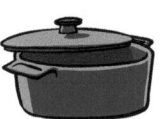

وعاء من الحديد

cast-iron pot

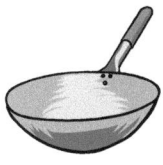

قدر صيني

wok / kadai

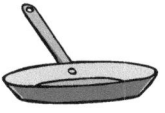

مقلاة

pan

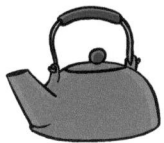

غلاية

kettle

قدر البخار

steamer

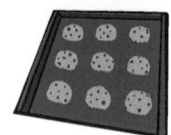

صينية

baking tray

أواني

crockery

فنجان

mug

صحن

bowl

عيدان الأكل

chopsticks

مغرفة

ladle

ملعقة منبسطة

spatula

خفاقة

whisk

مصفاة

strainer

مصفاة

sieve

مبشرة

grater

هاون

mortar

شواء

barbecue

موقد

open fire

لوح التقطيع

chopping board

نشّابة

rolling pin

مفتاح الزجاجات

corkscrew

علبة

can

مفتاح العلب المعدنية

can opener

قماش الفرن

pot holder

مجلى

sink

فرشاة

brush

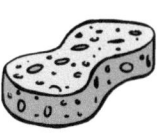

إسفنج

sponge

خلاط

blender

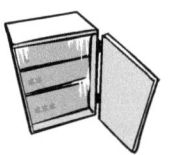

مجمّدة

deep freezer

زجاجة الطفل

baby bottle

صنبور الماء

tap

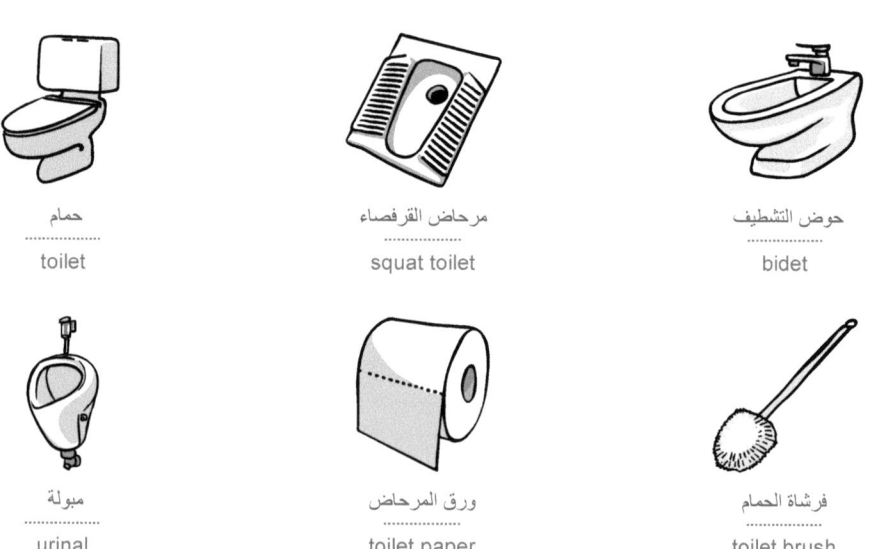

الحمّام

bathroom

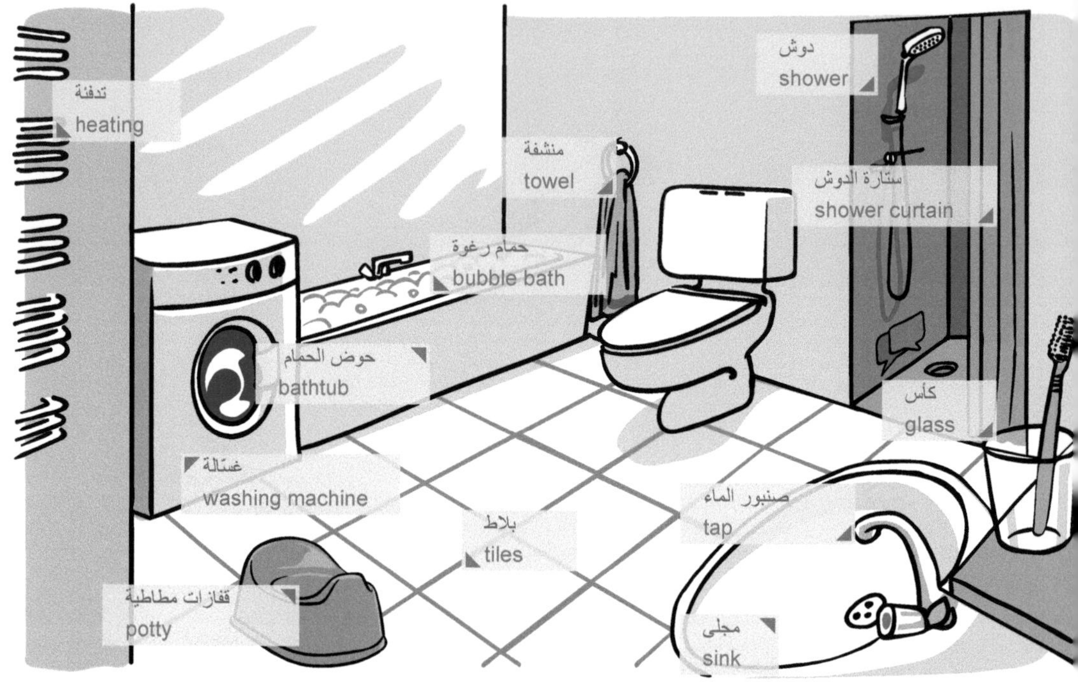

دوش
shower
تدفئة
heating
منشفة
towel
ستارة الدوش
shower curtain
حمام رغوة
bubble bath
حوض الحمام
bathtub
كأس
glass
غسّالة
washing machine
صنبور الماء
tap
بلاط
tiles
قفازات مطاطية
potty
مجلى
sink

حمام

toilet

مرحاض القرفصاء

squat toilet

حوض التشطيف

bidet

مبولة

urinal

ورق المرحاض

toilet paper

فرشاة الحمام

toilet brush

فرشاة الأسنان

toothbrush

معجون الأسنان

toothpaste

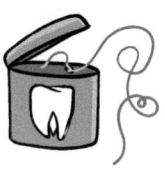

خيط حرير لتنظيف الأسنان

dental floss

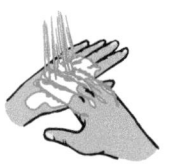

يغسل

wash

رشاش ماء يدوي

handheld shower

شطاف

douche

حوض الغسيل

basin

فرشاة الظهر

back brush

صابون

soap

جيل الدوش

shower gel

شامبو

shampoo

ممسحة

flannel

مصرف للماء

drain

مرهم

cream

مزيل الروائح

deodorant

مرآة

mirror

مرآة يد

hand mirror

موس حلاقة

razor

رغوة الحلاقة

shaving foam

كولونيا

aftershave

مشط

comb

فرشاة

brush

سشوار

hair dryer

مثبت للشعر

hairspray

ماكياج

makeup

روج

lipstick

طلاء أظافر

nail varnish

قطن

cotton wool

مقص أظافر

nail scissors

عطر

perfume

سلّة الغسيل

washbag

مقعد صغير

stool

ميزان

weighing scale

معطف الحمام

bathrobe

قفازات مطاطية

rubber gloves

سدادة قطنية

tampon

منشفة صحية

sanitary towel

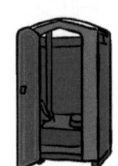

تواليت كيميائية

chemical toilet

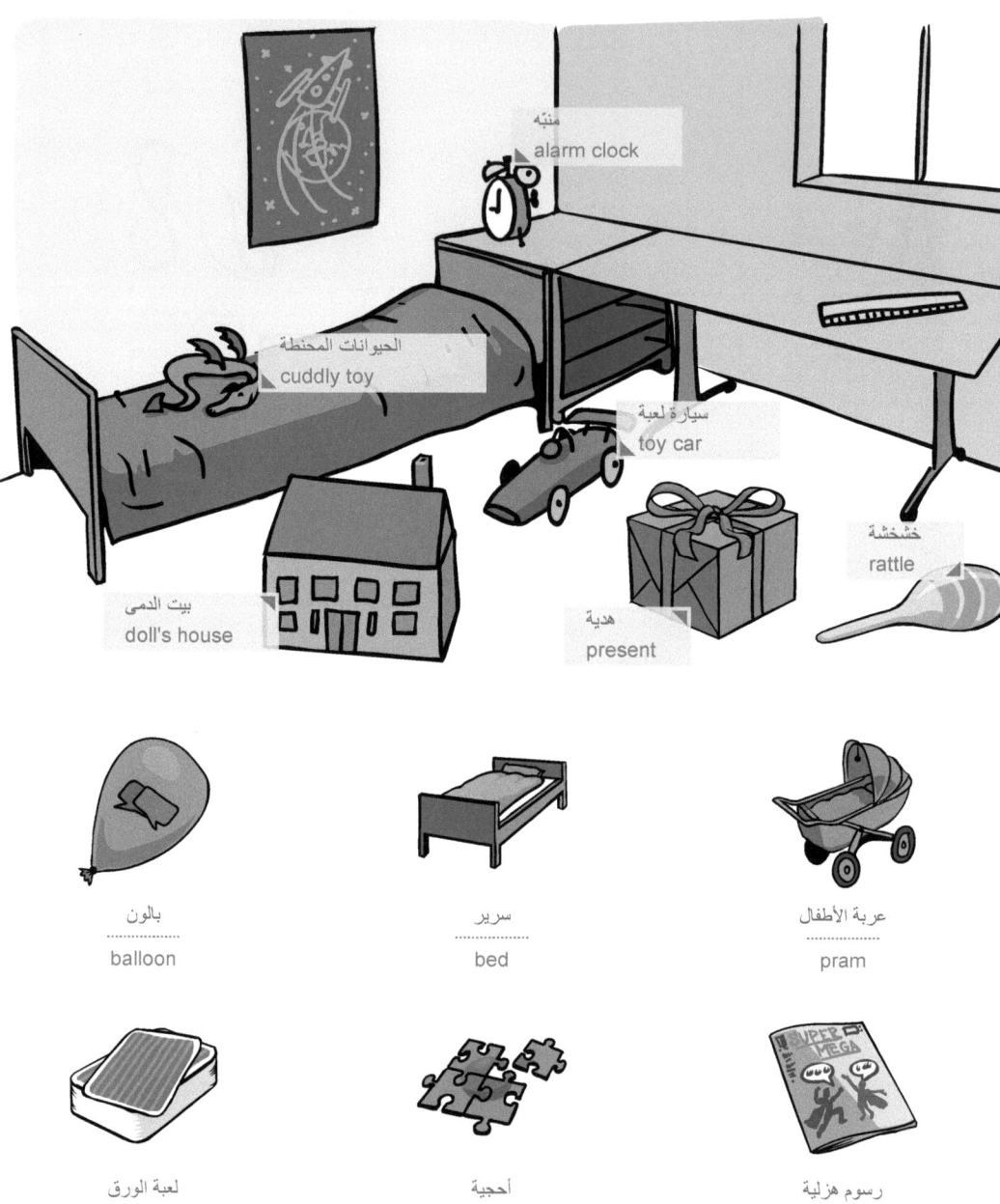

منبّه
alarm clock

الحيوانات المحنطة
cuddly toy

سيارة لعبة
toy car

خشخشة
rattle

بيت الدمى
doll's house

هدية
present

بالون
balloon

سرير
bed

عربة الأطفال
pram

لعبة الورق
deck of cards

أحجية
jigsaw

رسوم هزلية
comic

أحجار الليغو

lego bricks

حجارة تركيب

building blocks

دمية بطل

action figure

لباس الطفل

babygrow

فريسبي

frisbee

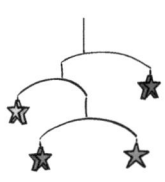

دمية معلّقة

mobile

لعبة الطاولة

board game

لعبة النرد

dice

لعبة قطار

model train set

مصّاصة

dummy

حفلة

party

كتاب مصوّر

picture book

كرة

ball

دمية

doll

يلعب

play

ملعب رملي للأطفال

sandpit

أرجوحة

swing

لعبة

toys

ألعاب فيديو

video game console

دراجة ثلاثية

tricycle

دمية على شكل الدب

teddy bear

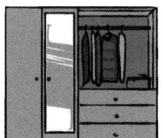

خزانة الثياب

wardrobe

ثياب

clothing

جوارب قصيرة

socks

جوارب طويلة

stockings

جورب بنطلون

tights

شال
scarf

شمسية
umbrella

تي شيرت
t-shirt

حزام
belt

حذاء شتوي
boots

شبشب
slippers

أحذية رياضية
trainers

صندل
sandals

حذاء
shoes

جزمة كاوتشوك
rubber boots

سروال داخلي
underpants

صدّارة
bra

قميص داخلي
vest

لباس ملاصق للجسم

body

بنطلون

trousers

جينز

jeans

تنورة

skirt

بلوزة

blouse

قميص

shirt

سترة قطنية

pullover

كنزة كم طويل

hoodie

سترة فضفاضة

blazer

سترة

jacket

معطف

coat

معطف مطري

raincoat

زي – طقم نسائي

costume

ثوب

dress

ثوب الزفاف

wedding dress

طقم

suit

قميص نوم

nightgown

بيجاما

pyjamas

ساري

sari

حجاب

headscarf

عمامة

turban

برقع

burqa

قفطان

kaftan

عباءة

abaya

مايوه

swimsuit

سروال سباحة

trunks

شرت

shorts

بدلة رياضية

tracksuit

مئزر

apron

ققازات

gloves

زر

button

نظّارة

glasses

إسوارة

bracelet

عِقد

necklace

خاتم

ring

قرط

earring

طاقِيّة

cap

علاقة ثياب

coat hanger

قُبَّعة

hat

ربطة العنق

tie

سحّاب

zip

خوذة

helmet

حمّالة البنطلون

braces

اللِباس المدرسي

school uniform

زيّ موحّد

uniform

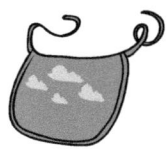

مريلة الأطفال

bib

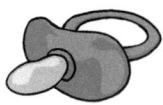

مصّاصة

dummy

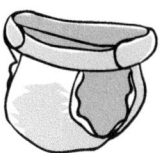

لفافة

nappy

مكتب

office

المخدّم
server
خزانة الملفات
filing cabinet
طابعة
printer
ورقة
paper
شاشة
monitor
فارة
mouse
طاولة المكتب
desk
ملف
folder
لوحة المفاتيح
keyboard
قماما
waste-paper basket
حاسوب
computer
كرسي
chair

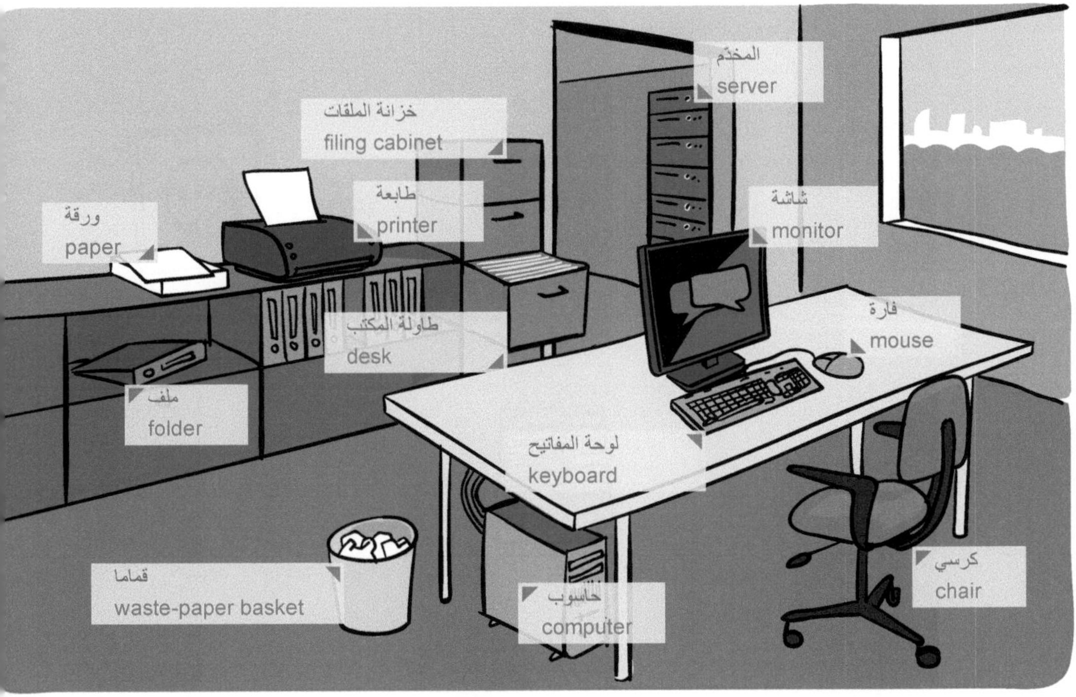

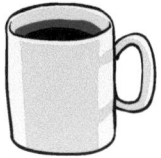

كأس من القهوة

coffee mug

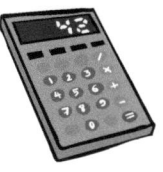

الآلة الحاسبة

calculator

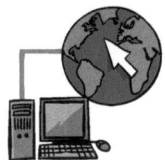

الإنترنت

internet

الحاسوب المحمول

laptop

رسالة

letter

خبر

message

الهاتف المحمول

mobile

شبكة

network

جهاز تصوير

photocopier

البرمجيات

software

هاتف

telephone

مقبس كهرباتي

plug socket

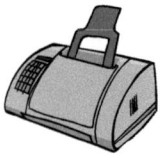

فاكس

fax machine

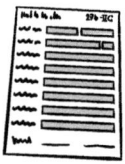

استمارة

form

وثيقة

document

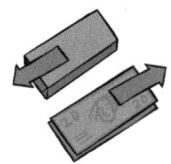

يشتري

buy

يدفع

pay

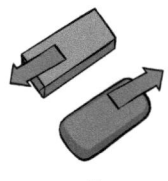

يتاجر

trade

مال

money

دولار

dollar

يورو

euro

ين

yen

روبل

rouble

فرنك سويسري

Swiss franc

يوان

renminbi yuan

روبية

rupee

صرّاف آلي

cashpoint

مكتب صرافة

bureau de change

ذهب

gold

فضة

silver

نفط

oil

طاقة

energy

سعر

price

عقد

contract

ضريبة

tax

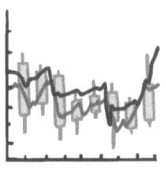

سهم

stock

يعمل

work

موظف

employee

رب العمل

employer

مصنع

factory

متجر

shop

المِهَن

occupations

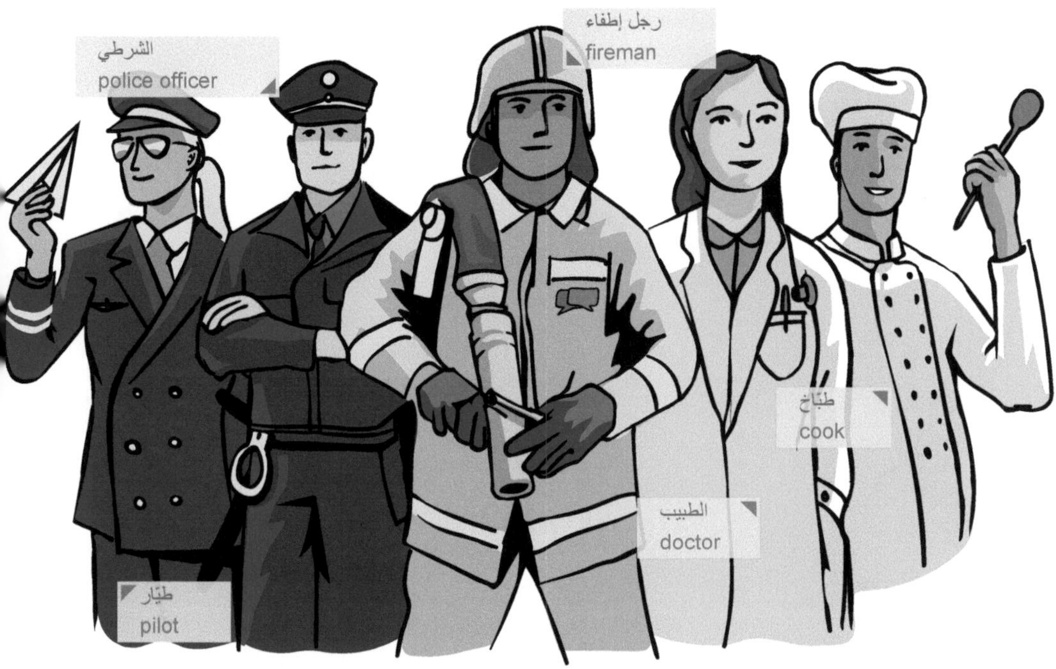
رجل إطفاء
fireman
الشرطي
police officer
طبّاخ
cook
الطبيب
doctor
طيّار
pilot

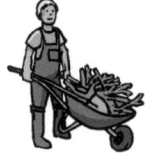

بستاني

gardener

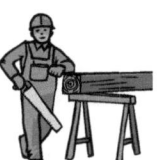

نجّار

carpenter

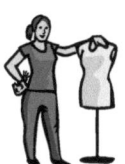

خيّاطة

seamstress

قاض

judge

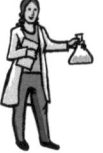

كيميائي

chemist

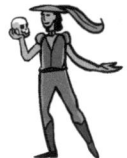

ممثل

actor

سائق حافلة

bus driver

سائق تاكسي

taxi driver

صياد سمك

fisherman

أجيرة للتنظيف

cleaning lady

بنّاء سقف

roofer

نادل

waiter

صيّاد

hunter

رسّام

painter

خباز

baker

كهربائي

electrician

عامل بناء

builder

مهندس

engineer

لحّام

butcher

سمكري

plumber

ساعي البريد

postman

جندي

soldier

مهندس معماري

architect

أمين صندوق

cashier

بائع الزهور

florist

حلاق

hairdresser

مراقب القطار

conductor

ميكانيكي

mechanic

قبطان

captain

طبيب أسنان

dentist

رجل العلم

scientist

حاخام

rabbi

إمام

imam

راهب

monk

كاهن

clergyman

عدة عمل

tools

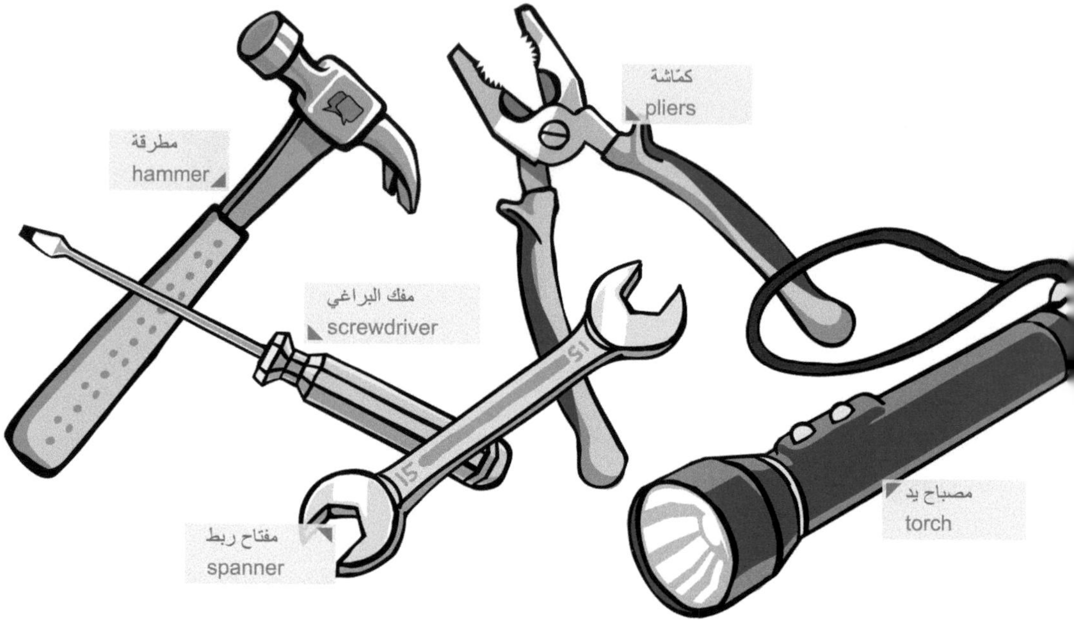

مطرقة
hammer
كمّاشة
pliers
مفك البراغي
screwdriver
مصباح يد
torch
مفتاح ربط
spanner

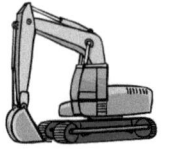

جرافة

digger

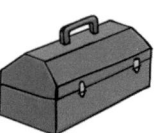

صندوق العدة

toolbox

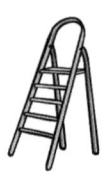

سلّم

ladder

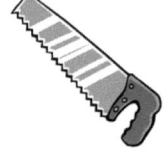

منشار

saw

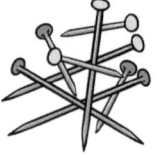

مسامير

nails

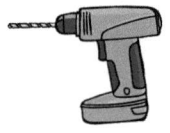

مثقب

drill

يصلح

repair

مجرفة

shovel

اللعنة

Damn!

لقاطة الكناسة

dustpan

سطل الألوان

paint pot

براغي

screws

آلات موسيقية

musical instruments

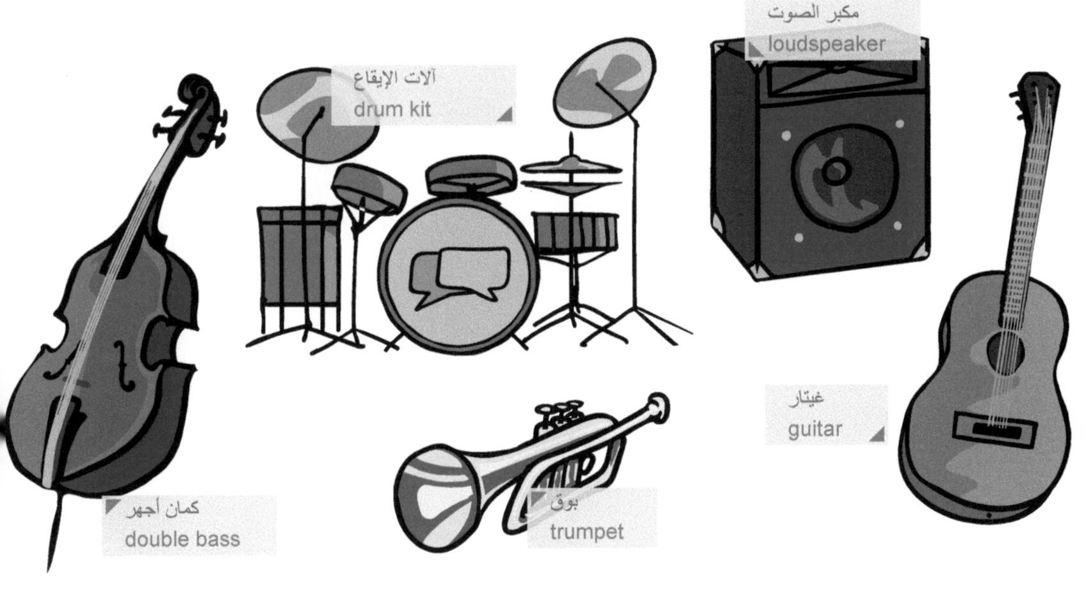

آلات الإيقاع
drum kit

مكير الصوت
loudspeaker

غيتار
guitar

كمان أجهر
double bass

بوق
trumpet

بيانو

piano

كمنجة

violin

جهير

bass

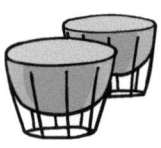

طبل كبير

timpani

طبل

drums

بيانو كهربائي

keyboard

ساكسوفون

saxophone

ناي

flute

ميكروفون

microphone

حديقة حيوانات

ZOO

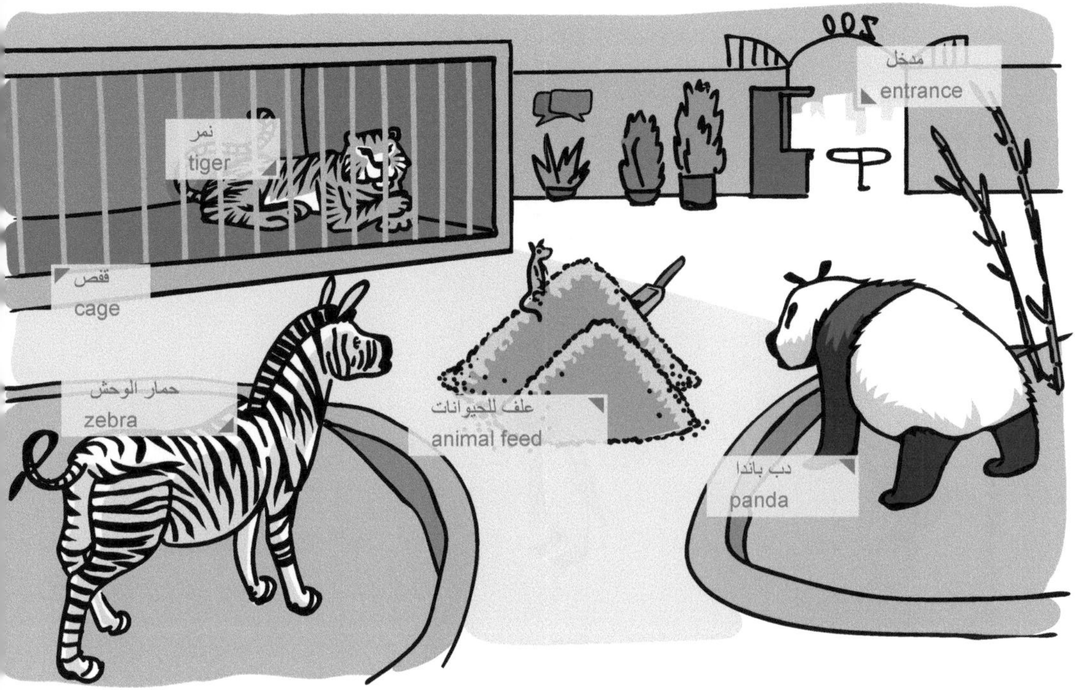

نمر
tiger
مدخل
entrance
قفص
cage
حمار الوحش
zebra
علف للحيوانات
animal feed
دب باندا
panda

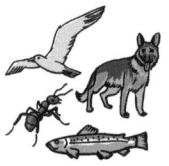

حيوانات

animals

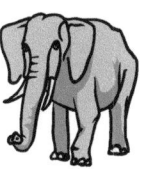

فيل

elephant

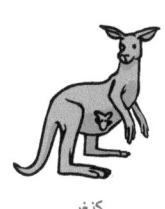

كنغر

kangaroo

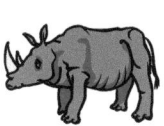

وحيد القرن

rhino

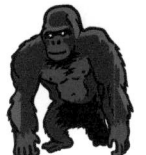

غوريلا

gorilla

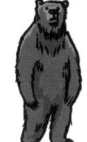

دب

bear

جمل

camel

نعامة

ostrich

أسد

lion

قرد

monkey

طائر فلامينغو

flamingo

ببغاء

parrot

دب قطبي

polar bear

بطريق

penguin

سمك القرش

shark

طاووس

peacock

أفعى

snake

تمساح

crocodile

حارس في حديقة الحيوان

zookeeper

عجل البحر

seal

نمر أمريكي مرقط

jaguar

فرس قزم

pony

نمر

leopard

فرس النهر

hippo

زرافة

giraffe

نسر

eagle

خنزير برّي

boar

سمك

fish

سلحفاة

turtle

حيوان فظ البحري

walrus

ثعلب

fox

غزال

gazelle

كرة القدم الأمريكية
American football

ركوب الدراجات
cycling

كرة التنس
tennis

كرة السلة
basketball

السباحة
swimming

الملاكمة
boxing

هوكي الجليد
ice hockey

كرة القدم
football

الريشة الطائرة
badminton

ألعاب القوى الخفيفة
athletics

كرة اليد
handball

التزلج على الثلج
skiing

بولو
polo

يَكتُب	يرسم	يُري
write	draw	show

يدفع	يعطي	يأخذ
push	give	take

يملك

have

يعمل

do

يوجد

be

يقف

stand

يركض

run

يسحب

pull

يرمي

throw

يقع

fall

يستلقي

lie

ينتظر

wait

يحمل

carry

يجلس

sit

يلبس

get dressed

ينام

sleep

يستيقظ

wake up

ينظر إلى ..
....
look at

يبكي
....
cry

يمسّد
....
stroke

يمشّط
....
comb

يتكلم
....
talk

يفهم
....
understand

يسأل
....
ask

يسمع
....
listen

يشرب
....
drink

ياكل
....
eat

يرتب
....
tidy up

يحب
....
love

يطبخ
....
cook

يقود
....
drive

يطير
....
fly

يبحر بزورق شراعي

sail

يحسب

calculate

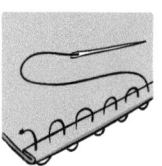

يقرأ

read

يتعلّم

learn

يعمل

work

يتزوج

marry

يخيط

sew

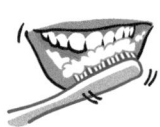

ينظف أسنانه

brush teeth

يقتّل

kill

يدخّن

smoke

يرسل

send

عائلة

family

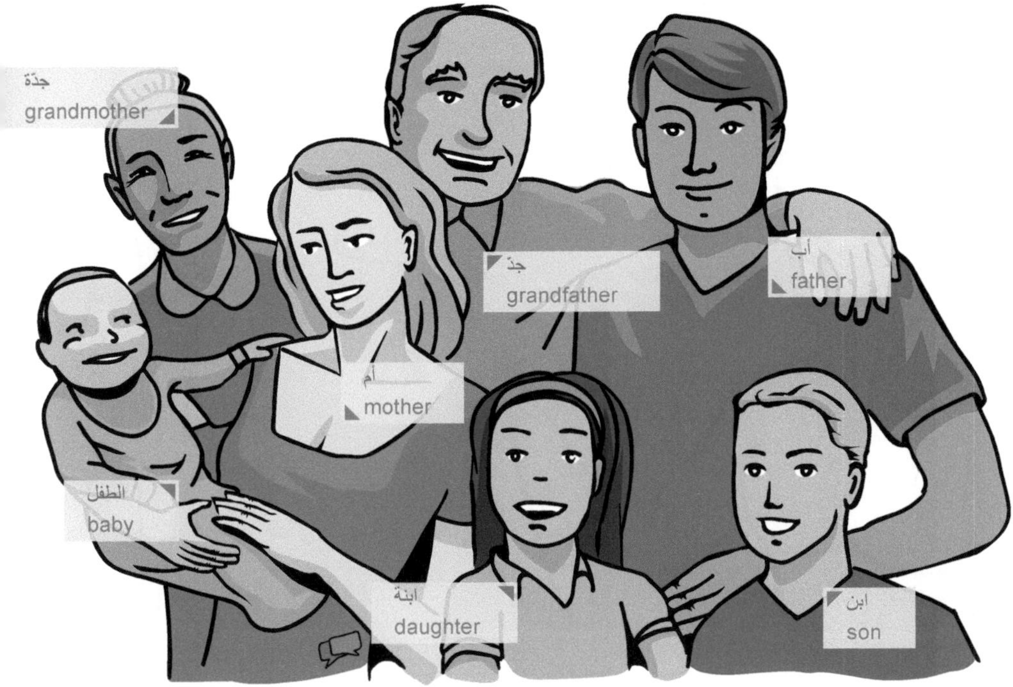
جدّة
grandmother
جدّ
grandfather
أب
father
أم
mother
الطفل
baby
ابنة
daughter
ابن
son

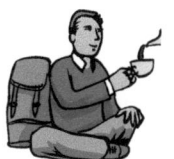

ضيف

guest

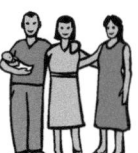

عمّة / خالة

aunt

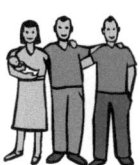

عمّ / خال

uncle

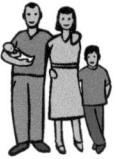

أخ

brother

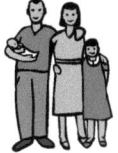

أخت

sister

الجسم

body

الجبين
forehead
العين
eye
الكتف
shoulder
الإصبع
finger
الوجه
face
الذقن
chin
اليد
hand
الساق
leg
الصدر
breast
الذراع
arm

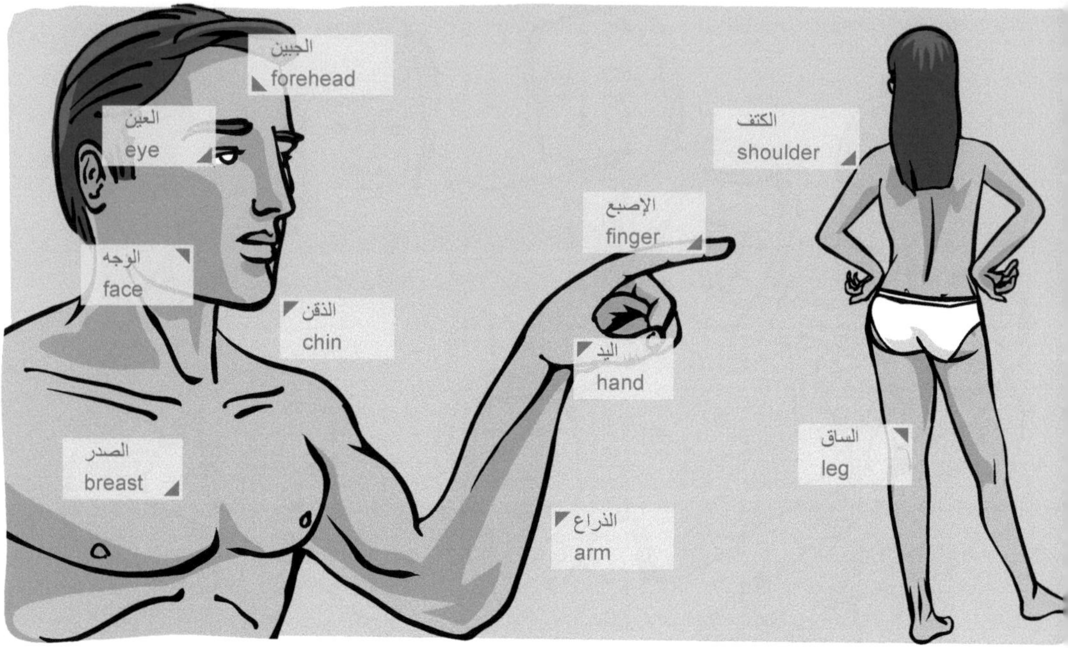

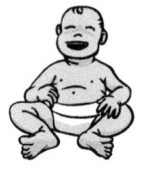

الطفل

baby

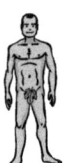

الرجل

man

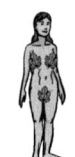

المرأة

woman

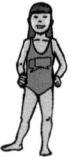

البنت

girl

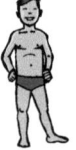

الولد

boy

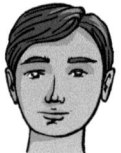

الرأس

head

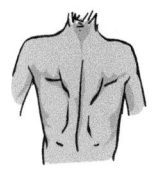

الظهر

back

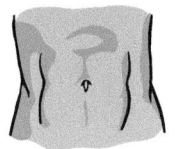

البطن

belly

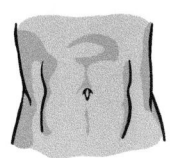

السرّة

belly button

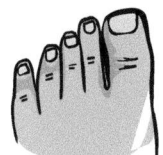

إصبع القدم

toe

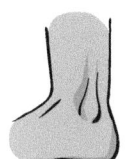

الكعب

heel

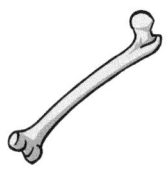

العظم

bone

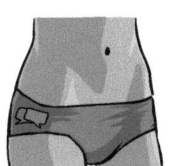

الورك

hip

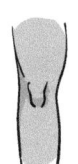

الركبة

knee

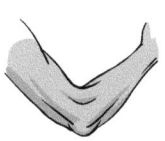

المرفق

elbow

الأَنف

nose

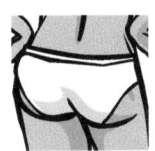

العَجُز

bottom

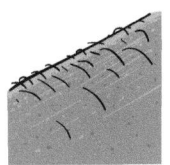

البَشرة

skin

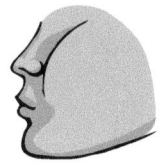

الخد

cheek

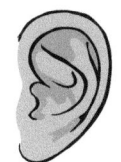

الأذن

ear

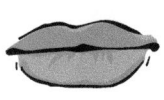

الشفة

lip

الفم

mouth

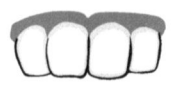

السن

tooth

اللسان

tongue

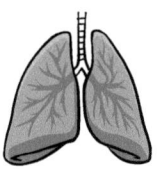

الدماغ

brain

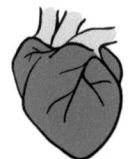

القلب

heart

العضلة

muscle

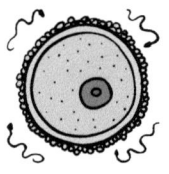

الرئة

lung

الكبد

liver

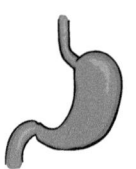

المعدة

stomach

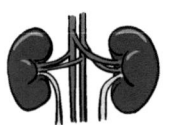

الكلى

kidneys

الاتصال الجنسي

sex

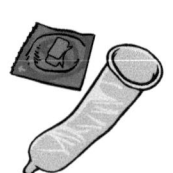

الواقي المطاطي

condom

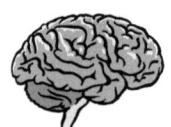

البويضة

ovum

المنيّ

semen

الحمل

pregnancy

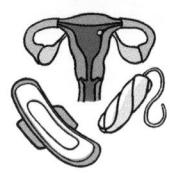

الحيض

menstruation

المهبل

vagina

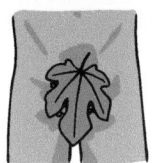

القضيب

penis

الحاجب

eyebrow

الشعر

hair

الرقبة

neck

المستشفى

hospital

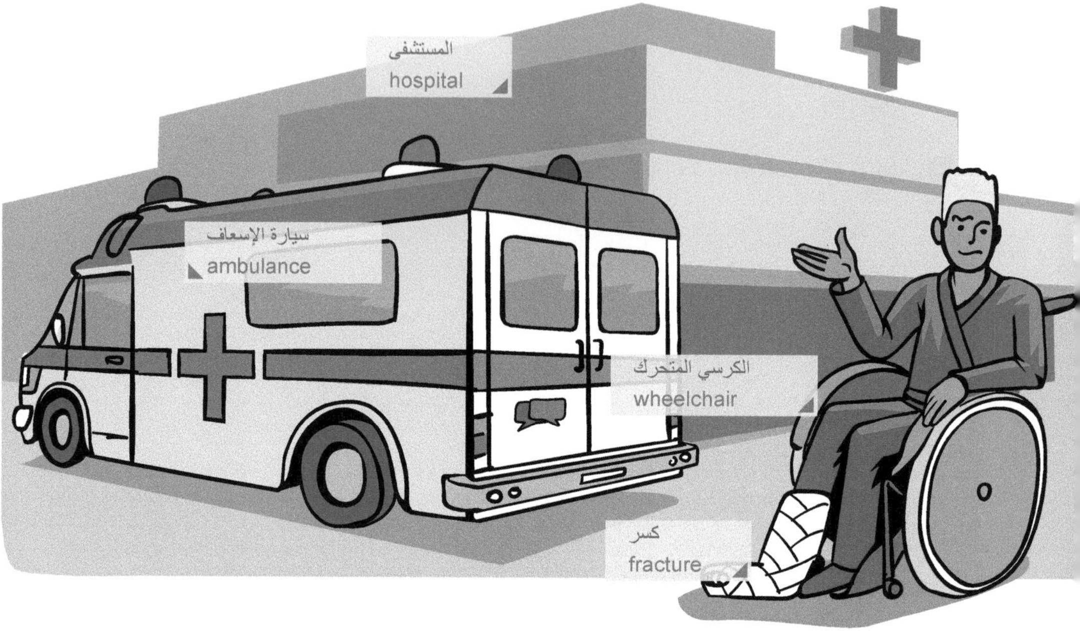

المستشفى
hospital
سيارة الإسعاف
ambulance
الكرسي المتحرك
wheelchair
كسر
fracture

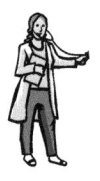

الطبيب

doctor

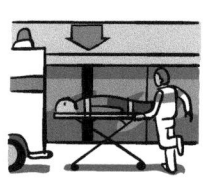

غرفة الإسعاف

emergency room

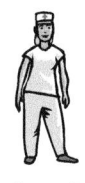

الممرضة

nurse

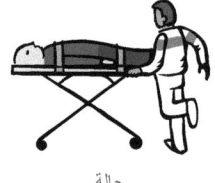

حالة

emergency

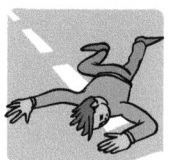

مغمى عليه

unconscious

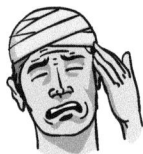

الألم

pain

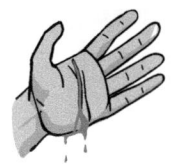

إصابة

injury

النزيف

bleeding

احتشاء القلب

heart attack

جلطة

stroke

حسسية

allergy

السعال

cough

الحُمّى

fever

إنفلونزا

flu

الإسهال

diarrhoea

وجع الرأس

headache

السرطان

cancer

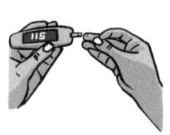

مرض السكر

diabetes

جرّاح

surgeon

مبضع

scalpel

عملية

operation

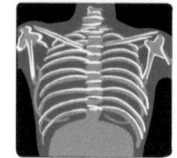

سيتي سكان

CT

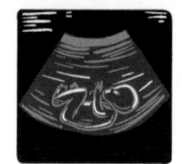

الأشعة السينية

x-ray

فوق الصوتي

ultrasound

القناع

face mask

المرض

disease

غرفة الانتظار

waiting room

العُكّاز

crutch

شريط لاصق

plaster

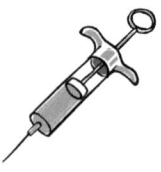

ضماد

bandage

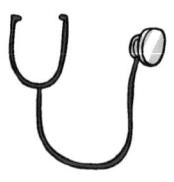

حقنة

injection

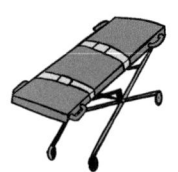

سمّاعة الطبيب

stethoscope

نقالة

stretcher

ميزان حرارة

clinical thermometer

ولادة

birth

وزن زائد

overweight

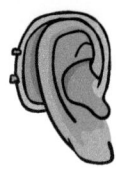

جهاز السمع

hearing aid

المواد المعقمة

disinfectant

عدوى

infection

فيروس

virus

الإيدز

HIV / AIDS

الطب

medicine

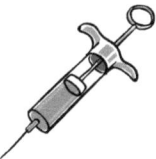

اللقاح

vaccination

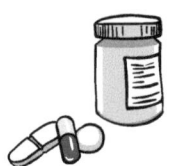

أقراص الدواء

tablets

حبّة الدواء

pill

نداء النجدة

emergency call

مقياس ضغط الدم

blood pressure monitor

مريض / صحيح

ill / healthy

النجدة!
....
Help!

إنذار
....
alarm

اعتداء
....
assault

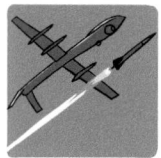

هجوم
....
attack

خطر
....
danger

مخرج طوارئ
....
emergency exit

حريق!
....
Fire!

جهاز الإطفاء
....
fire extinguisher

حادث
....
accident

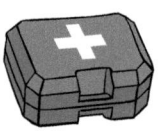

حقيبة الإسعاف الأولي
....
first-aid kit

أنقذونا
....
SOS

الشرطة
....
police

أوروبا

Europe

أمريكا الشمالية

North America

أمريكا الجنوبية

South America

أفريقيا

Africa

آسيا

Asia

أستراليا

Australia

المحيط الأطلسي

Atlantic

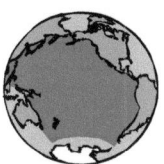

المحيط الهادي

Pacific

المحيط الهندي

Indian Ocean

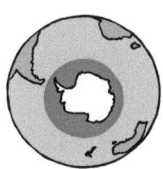

المحيط المتجمد الجنوبي

Antarctic Ocean

المحيط المتجمد الشمالي

Arctic Ocean

القطب الشمالي

North Pole

القطب الجنوبي

South Pole

منطقة القطب الجنوبي

Antarctica

أرض

Earth

بر

land

بحر

sea

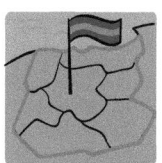

جزيرة

island

أمة

nation

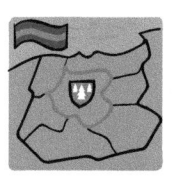

دولة

state

ميناء الساعة

clock face

عقرب الساعات

hour hand

عقرب الدقائق

minute hand

عقرب الثواني

second hand

كم الساعة الآن؟

What time is it?

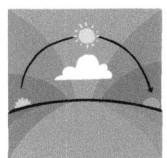

يوم

day

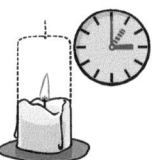

زمن

time

الآن

now

ساعة رقمية

digital watch

دقيقة

minute

ساعة

hour

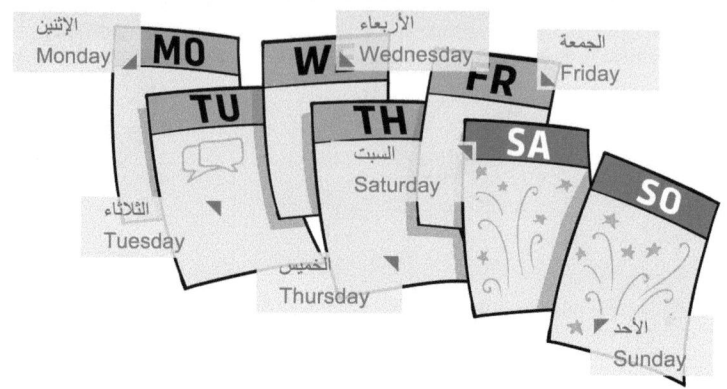

الإثنين
Monday

الأربعاء
Wednesday

الجمعة
Friday

الثلاثاء
Tuesday

الخميس
Thursday

السبت
Saturday

الأحد
Sunday

الأمس

yesterday

اليوم

today

غدًا

tomorrow

الصباح

morning

الظهر

noon

المساء

evening

MO	TU	WE	TH	FR	SA	SU
1	2	3	4	5	6	7
8	9	10	11	12	13	14
15	16	17	18	19	20	21
22	23	24	25	26	27	28
29	30	31	1	2	3	4

أيام العمل

business days

MO	TU	WE	TH	FR	SA	SU
1	2	3	4	5	6	7
8	9	10	11	12	13	14
15	16	17	18	19	20	21
22	23	24	25	26	27	28
29	30	31	1	2	3	4

نهاية الأسبوع

weekend

سنة
year

مطر
rain
قوس قزح
rainbow
ريح
wind
ثلج
snow
الربيع
spring
الخريف
autumn
الصيف
summer
الشتاء
winter

4.APRIL 11°
5.APRIL 4°
6.APRIL 13°
7.APRIL 8°
8.APRIL 10°

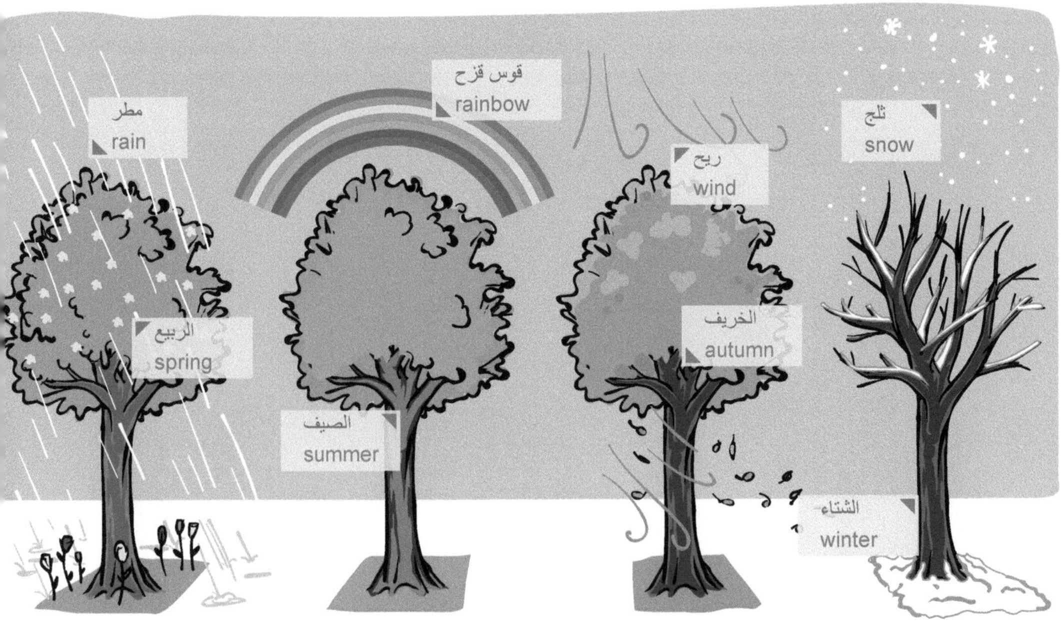

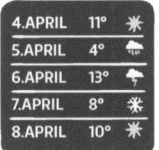

التنبؤ بالحالة الجوية
....
weather forecast

F C
120 90 60 30 0 -30
40 30 20 10 0 -10 -20

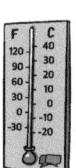

مقياس حرارة
....
thermometer

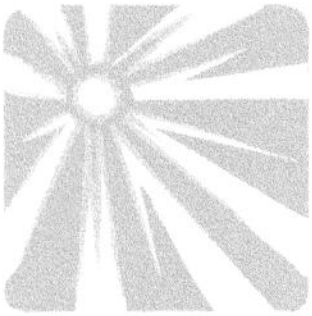

ضوء الشمس
....
sunshine

سحابة
....
cloud

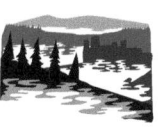

ضباب
....
fog

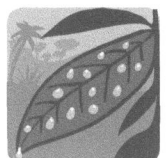

رطوبة الجو
....
humidity

برق

lightning

رعد

thunder

عاصفة

storm

بَرَد

hail

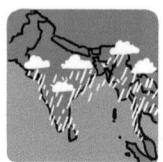

ريح موسمية

monsoon

طوفان

flood

جليد

ice

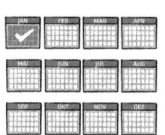

كانون الثاني / يناير

January

شباط / فبراير

February

آذار / مارس

March

نيسان / أبريل

April

أيار / مايو

May

حزيران / يونيو

June

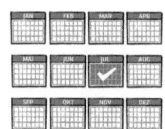

تموز / يوليو

July

آب / أغسطس

August

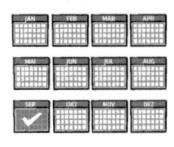

أيلول / سبتمبر

September

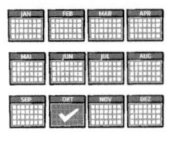

تشرين الأول / أكتوبر

October

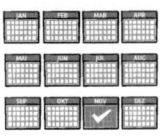

تشرين الثاني / نوفمبر

November

كانون الأول / ديسمبر

December

أشكال

shapes

دائرة

circle

مربّع

square

مستطيل

rectangle

مثلّث

triangle

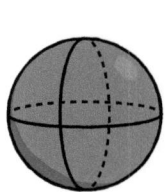

كرة

sphere

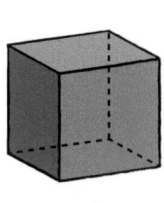

مكعب

cube

أبيض

white

أصفر

yellow

برتقالي

orange

وردي

pink

أحمر

red

بنفسجي

purple

أزرق

blue

أخضر

green

بني

brown

رمادي

grey

أسود

black

كثير / قليل

a lot / a little

غضبان / هادئ

angry / calm

جميل / قبيح

beautiful / ugly

بداية / نهاية

beginning / end

كبير / صغير

big / small

فاتح / قاتم

bright / dark

أخ / أخت

brother / sister

نظيف / وسخ

clean / dirty

كامل / ناقص

complete / incomplete

نهار / ليل

day / night

ميت / حيّ

dead / alive

عريض / ضيّق

wide / narrow

صالح للأكل / غير صالح

edible / inedible

شرّير / لطيف

evil / kind

مثير / ممل

excited / bored

سمين / نحيف

fat / thin

أولاً / أخيراً

first / last

صديق / عدو

friend / enemy

مليء / فارغ

full / empty

صلب / لين

hard / soft

ثقيل / خفيف

heavy / light

جوع / عطش

hunger / thirst

مريض / صحيح

ill / healthy

غير شرعي / شرعي

illegal / legal

ذكي / غبي

intelligent / stupid

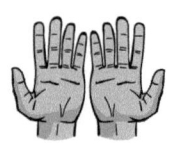

يسار / يمين

left / right

قريب / بعيد

near / far

جديد / مستعمل

new / used

لا شيء / بعض الشيء

nothing / something

مسين / شاب

old / young

يشعل / يطفئ

on / off

مفتوح / مغلق

open / closed

خافت / عالٍ

quiet / loud

غني / فقير

rich / poor

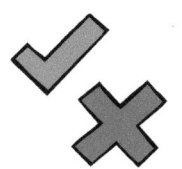

صح / خطأ

right / wrong

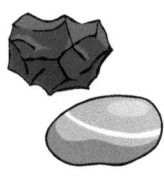

أحرش / املس

rough / smooth

حزين / سعيد

sad / happy

قصير / طويل

short / long

بطيء / سريع

slow / fast

مبلول / جاف

wet / dry

ساخن / بارد

warm / cool

حرب / سلم

war / peace

0

صفر

zero

1

واحد

one

2

اثنان

two

3

ثلاثة

three

4

أربعة

four

5

خمسة

five

6

ستة

six

7

سبعة

seven

8

ثمانية

eight

9

تسعة

nine

10

عشرة

ten

11

أحد عشر

eleven

12

اثنا عشر

twelve

13

ثلاثة عشر

thirteen

14

أربعة عشر

fourteen

15

خمسة عشر

fifteen

16

ستة عشر

sixteen

17

سبعة عشر

seventeen

18

ثمانية عشر

eighteen

19

تسعة عشر

nineteen

20

عشرون

twenty

100

مائة

hundred

1.000

ألف

thousand

1.000.000

مليون

million

languages

الإنكليزية

English

الإنكليزية الأمريكية

American English

لغة ماندارين الصينية

Chinese Mandarin

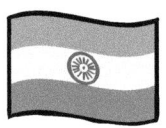

الهندية

Hindi

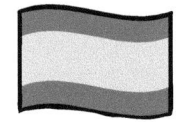

الإسبانية

Spanish

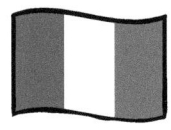

الفرنسية

French

العربية

Arabic

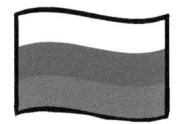

الروسية

Russian

البرتغالية

Portuguese

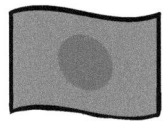

البنغالية

Bengali

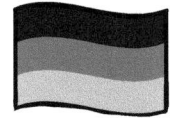

الألمانية

German

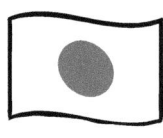

اليابانية

Japanese

أنا
....
I

أنت
....
you

هو / هي
....
he / she / it

نحن
....
we

أنتم
....
you

هم
....
they

من؟
....
who?

ماذا؟
....
what?

كيف؟
....
how?

أين؟
....
where?

متى؟
....
when?

اسم
....
name

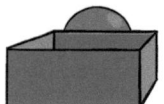

خلف
....
behind

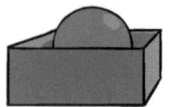

في
....
in

أمام
....
in front of

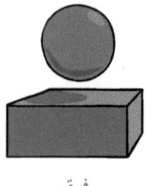

فوق
....
over

على
....
on

تحت
....
under

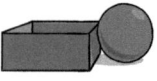

جنب
....
beside

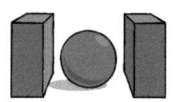

بين
....
between

مكان
....
place